1999

POWERBOATS

BOATS & SHIPS

Jason Cooper

The Rourke Corporation, Inc.
Vero Beach, Florida 32964

© 1999 The Rourke Corporation, Inc.

PHOTO CREDITS:
courtesy Fountain Boats: page 4, 8; © Paul Kemiel: cover, title page, pages 10, 12-13, 15, 17, 18, 21; courtesy Pacific Trawlers: page 7

CREATIVE SERVICES:
East Coast Studios, Merritt Island, Florida

EDITORIAL SERVICES:
Susan Albury

Library of Congress Cataloging-in-Publication Data

Cooper, Jason, 1942-
    Power boats / by Jason Cooper.
      p. cm. — (Boats)
    Includes index.
    Summary: Surveys the uses, parts, and different kinds of power boats.
    ISBN 0-86593-564-5
    1. Motorboats—Juvenile literature.
[1. Motorboats.]
I. Title II. Series: Cooper, Jason, 1942- Boats & ships
GV835.C66   1999
623.8' 231—dc21   99–15114
                                 CIP

Printed in the USA

TABLE OF CONTENTS

POWERBOATS

Many different kinds of boats are used for fishing, waterskiing, diving, cruising, and racing. They are all pleasure boats, and most of them are motorboats.

Sometimes the pleasure boats with motors are called powerboats. The term *power boat,* though, is best used for high-powered racing boats.

Most pleasure boats are less than 20 feet (6 meters) long. Small, quick boats called **runabouts** (RUH nuh bauts), for example, are usually 14 to 16 feet (4.3-4.9 meters) long.

Twin outboard engines give this pleasure boat plenty of power.

A larger type of pleasure boat is the cabin cruiser. A cabin cruiser has a raised, roofed area called the cabin. It holds the boat controls and places to sit and eat. Below the cabin are sleeping quarters.

Yachts (YAHTS) are large motorboats. They can cost several million dollars.

Ocean liners and other big **vessels** (VEH sulz) are called ships. Ships that aren't armed with guns for fighting are built to carry freight or large numbers of passengers.

This powerful motor yacht of the trawler type is built to handle ocean travel.

RACING BOATS

True powerboats are racing boats. Their smooth lines and big engines make them the muscle boats of lakes, rivers, and oceans. They are sleek and low, boats built for speed. Many of them look like jet fighter planes without wings.

There are many kinds of racing boats, most of them 11 to 20 feet (3.4-6.1 meters) long. All of them have sharply pointed **bows** (BOWZ), or fronts.

True powerboats are more than motorboats to many people. Powerboats are speedsters, built for racing.

RACING BOAT HULLS

The floating shell of any boat is its hull. The shape of the hull helps decide what the boat can do in the water. The sharp bow of racing boats, for example, helps them knife easily through the water.

Some racing hulls are designed to skim over the water when the boat is at high speed. These boats are known as **hydroplanes** (HI druh planez). They throw up great rooster tails of white water as they race at speeds up to 200 miles per hour (320 kilometers per hour).

Vrrrooom! Knifelike hulls of offshore racing boats slice up the Gulf of Mexico off Fort Meyers, Florida.

A tunnel hull boat with an outboard engine thunders across a lake. Tunnel hulls can still turn sharply at 140 miles per hour (225 kilometers per hour).

Other racing hulls ride in the water. Some of these boats, called flat bottoms, have slightly curved sides and a flat bottom.

Tunnel hull boats have two long floats. One is attached to each side of the lower hull. The floats create a tunnel along the length of the boat's bottom.

V-bottom hulls have a steeply slanted side. The V-bottom is designed for ocean racing. The V-shape helps a boat smash through rough water.

A V-hull racing boat has a steeply slanted side to help it dash through ocean water at speeds up to 150 miles per hour (240 kilometers per hour).

ENGINES AND PROPELLERS

A racing boat is more than a hull, of course. Its engine and propeller make it go.

Racing boats usually have one engine. However, some offshore racing boats have as many as four.

In some racing classes, boats use an inboard engine. **Inboards** (IN bordz) are placed inside the hull. Boats in **outboard** (OUT bord) classes have outboard engines, usually placed in sight on the **stern** (STURN), or rear, of the boats.

At the beginning of a formula one tunnel boat race, outboard engines fire up and soak starter crews. Most races begin from floating docks.

Inboards are usually automobile engines. A few, however, are aircraft engines. Outboards are designed only for boats. They're true marine engines.

Some classes of racing allow racers to modify, or change, their engines in ways to make them more powerful. Other classes use **stock** (STAHK) engines. Stock engines must remain the way the factory built them.

A propeller is powered by the boat's engine. As in any motorboat with a propeller, it churns in the water like fan blades. That motion pushes the boat forward.

This twin-hulled racer, of a type called a catamaran, is powered by four inboard automobile engines. Each kicks out about 1,000 horsepower!

19

POWERBOAT RACING

Powerboat racing in North America is a growing sport. The American Power Boat Association began a racing program in the United States in 1903. Today, over 200 boating clubs belong to the APBA. The group operates more than 300 racing events.

The APBA is part of an international powerboat association called the Union of International Motorboating. Canada's powerboat group, the Canadian Boating Federation, is also a member.

Unlimited hydroplanes are the fastest of power boats. They can race at speeds of 200 miles per hour (320 kilometers per hour).

The APBA has racing in 11 categories, or groups, such as offshore racing. Within each group are several classes. Each class offers racing for boats of different weights, shapes, and engine sizes.

A junior racing category allows young people a chance to race against each other as early as age nine. The J-class racers compete in both hydroplane and runabout classes.

Safety is extremely important in powerboat racing. Racers must wear life jackets and safety helmets.

GLOSSARY

bow (BOW) — the front portion of a boat or ship

hull (HUHL) — the floating shell of a boat or ship

hydroplane (HI druh plane) — a boat designed so that its hull is wholly or partly out of the water at high speeds

inboard (IN bord) — an engine that is placed in a ship's hull

outboard (OUT bord) — an engine designed for boats and placed outside the boat's hull, usually on the stern

runabout (RUH nuh baut) — a small, quick motorboat used for pleasure

stern (STURN) — the rear portion of a boat or ship

stock (STAHK) — refers to an engine that is factory-built and is not changed in any way

vessel (VEH sul) — a boat or ship

yacht (YAHT) — a large, expensive motorboat, usually 30 or more feet (9 meters) in length

INDEX

FURTHER READING

Find out more about power boats with these helpful information sites:

- Canadian Boating Federation (Federation Nautique du Canada), 50 Rue Jacques Cartier J6T 4R3, Valley Field, Quebec, Canada
- American Power Boat Association on line at apba-boatracing.com
- Offshore Racing Association on line at www.apba-offshore.com
- Union of International Motorboating on line at www.powerboating.com
- Unlimited Hydroplane Racing Association on line at www.uhra.com